THE MASK

THE MASK

I AM A SPIRITUAL BEING IN A HUMAN BODY

SALLY ANNE SAINT

Copyright © Sally Anne Saint 2020

Sally Anne Saint has asserted her right to be identified as the author of this Work in accordance with the Copyright, Designs and Patents Act 1988.

All rights reserved.
No part of this publication may be reproduced, stored in a retrieval system, or transmitted in any form or by any means, electronic, mechanical, photocopying, recording or otherwise, without the prior permission of the copyright owner.

Typeset by Fuzzy Flamingo
www.fuzzyflamingo.co.uk

A catalogue for this book is available from the British Library.

I dedicate this book to two people, to my son Edward who shone pure light and love on me from the very moment he entered my life, he is my greatest teacher. To my dear mum, Heather, who gave me life and love, she is always in my heart. Thank you my mum xxxx

I AM A SPIRITUAL BEING IN A HUMAN BODY

If that is so, then why is my pulse racing?

Why am I so ultra-aware of every job that needs doing, every single minute movement around me?

Every single word spoken around me?

Why am I a ball of anxiety?

And why is my mind running away with me?

Why?

FOREWORD

How many of us wear the perfect mask – the perfect life, and the perfect family – while inside, we are suffering in pain, anger and hurt?

We try so hard to push it all deep down, hoping it will disappear or at least not show in our world. The Mask protects us — or do we think it protects others from seeing our pain? Maybe it is a combination of both.

However, the hurt, pain and anger cannot be hidden. Often, it manifests itself in our choices and actions, and in the worry and insecurity we often feel. Pain and trauma from our past, including post-traumatic stress disorder (PTSD), can stop us in our tracks, letting us see only what caused us to feel damaged.

The Mask is the perfect book for anyone suffering

from the past or thinking of stepping into the journey of healing. Sally Saint bravely stepped into her own journey of healing — as she says, "peeling back the onion." Her book is reflective and powerfully insightful. It is extremely easy to find yourself relating to everything Sally talks about, stepping through one level, then another, slowly and steadily healing each layer until she feels whole, safe, and at peace.

Sally Saint's vulnerability and pure honesty is refreshing and extremely helpful to all those thinking of joining her on the journey of healing.

There are so many books out on the market that *tell* you how to heal. *The Mask* invites you to *feel* and *move* with ease into the healing journey. Why? Because doing so lets you experience and benefit from another person's experience. You're not alone.

And here is a secret: once we begin, we not only heal the hurt, we find our truth! This truth liberates you, breaks the chains of the past, and transforms you as you begin to feel whole!

Sally Saint has given this world a gift in *The Mask*. Thank you, Sally!

— Alena Chapman

PROLOGUE

When I gave birth to my son, I was completely and utterly overwhelmed with a love that beamed onto and into every part of my being. This child emitted the radiance of unconditional love and it was truly divine.

It was something that just flowed from this little being, fresh from the world that we all came from – Spirit. For every single child that is born reminds us of this truth; they beam the energy from where they originated and they remind us of our home. Where unconditional love is the norm, where there is only this love.

Yet over time our connection to spirit becomes eroded and we focus more and more on the physical, on that which is outside of us and that which others have. We move from the space of love and headlong into the world of lack and fear.

How do we know we are disconnected? When our mind feeds us illusions, illusions that are laced with fear. For when we are in balance, our minds have a healthy attitude, about ourselves and about others. Place the disconnection inside and the mind turns on itself and us.

For if we truly believe all the fear, all the self-destroying chatter, then we are truly lost.

Here comes in the role of 'The Mask', the face we put on that hides what we are really feeling and hides who we truly are. The Mask is made up of others' opinions, ideas, any conforming influence and any pressure. All of which create a unique hiding place.

Fear feeds and keeps 'The Mask' in place.

'The Mask' hides us from others but also from ourselves; denial of our true selves hides and buries our originality. We start to accept this hiding and the illusion of self.

Begin the path of removing 'The Mask'

CHAPTER ONE

22/10/18 THE BEGINNING

At the thought of writing this, my very first book, my mind played tricks. There was this massive resistance, there was the negative mind chatter telling me that there was no way on earth I could do this. Why would anyone want to read my book and my words? It was so convincing. Then there was this physical anxiety, an avoidance strategy that came immediately out to play; the ultimate goal being that I never actually start the project in the first place.

Even now, right at this very moment that I am writing these words, my head is doing its very best to stop the process. When I misspell something, or rewrite a sentence, it is doing its very best to stop me.

Yet here I am, I am starting. Sitting on my sofa, looking out at my washing blowing gently in the breeze, the sun is shining. It's a clear autumn day.

My eight-year-old son is sitting on the floor just in front of me, playing imaginary games with his Lego figures. To my right on my guest's chair is my mother, eighty-four years old, fast asleep. With a blanket on her body, the deep red and pink checks of the pattern wrap her up safe and warm. She looks tired, but peaceful, for she sleeps deep. Under her left elbow is the heart-shaped cushion that I found in a charity shop and by her right arm is a massive Minion toy that my son won at tenpin bowling.

There are candles, incense, books, toys, pieces of Lego everywhere, just waiting for the well known and loved Lego-related injuries to occur!

I want to remember every moment and be able to recall this, the first time, the very first time, and for those I love to be remembered as being here. Being here at the start of this new journey for me. For everything changes. My son grows taller and taller, my mother's body ages, she forgets more and more. Yet right now, in this very moment, it feels like the most precious gift. The gift being that they are here with me, beside me and we are all surrounded by peace.

Tears are in my eyes, tears of joy, yes, and then my mind kicks in with the record, the stuck record that replays the same pattern. My mother is ill and frail, she has tests this week at the hospital. What will happen? Will she be okay? What is going on? The mind has come out to play and it is leading me down a path, the path of worry for the future, something that cannot be predicted and something that fills absolutely no purpose, other than removing me from the gift of now, that which has been given, the gift of today.

How many times have I robbed myself of the very day I am in, by reliving my past and worrying about my future? How much time do I actually live in the now? If we all stepped back and viewed ourselves, we would be surprised.

I had a dream last night and it ripped through me, as it felt so real and incredibly intense, and I was woken from it. The dream was I was walking in some fields and in one was some loose horses, they looked like war horses. The soldiers were trying to catch them to remount, one galloped past me and I grabbed a leather strap that was around its neck; it stopped.

As I went to hand the horse back over to the soldier, I then saw I was surrounded by a ring of horses, all war horses and they were not happy, it became clear they wanted to attack me. So, I ran. I got to a safe building, got others in with me and, as we looked outside, we saw more and more people were being infected by this war energy of the horses and they were all looking for blood.

Like the zombies that are so often in films, I was living my own version of these made-up blood-seeking monsters in my night time dreaming. In the safe house was a room. My father was there and whoever had been nursing him thought he was recovering, that he had been infected but that he was coming out of the other side. As I neared the room, it became apparent he hadn't. He was vomiting and vomiting. With a heavy heart I stepped back from the door; it was too late.

I stepped back to the room of healthy people, where a woman suddenly showed signs and transformed into this being out for blood. The only weapon I had to stop her was a pencil, so I thrust through her open mouth. Her teeth had already changed to the canines of the predator. I pushed the pencil right through her mouth and up into the roof of it.

I was then shown a helicopter that was protected. It had red attachments glowing on it. I was put inside of it and instructed that the only way I could fly the helicopter was to bring my mind in-line with flight. It was the only way I would fly.

When I was woken, I could barely think, or drag myself together, so I lay there, let the morning, my son, the dog gradually set my body back into some function.

I understood a big part of the dream, for the messages in my life were showing me the fact that PTSD was making a big entrance into my life. The soldiers and war horses in my dream were showing me the truth about those who battle. They have something inside them that eats away at them and ultimately at others. Wherever I went and however much I tried to protect myself and others, this illness came too and transformed every situation. Fear was in its wake and in its being was fear.

As I write, the significance of me thrusting a pencil into the mouth of the final woman who attacked me showed me the way forwards. For you write with a pencil, you write. Here I am writing this book, after this dream. The final straw, the final symbolic version of myself, to keep transforming into the mental monster that destroys, that's enough.

The helicopter that symbolises flight can only take off by me balancing my mind with that of flight. What greater message did I need from Spirit to encourage me on this new journey. It is for my healing, for my father's healing, for males and females, for young and old, that I write this book. For all the silent traumas that no one knew of, the ones that were the dirty secrets, the ones that so affected us that now we see that we are the walking wounded. The only way we can be free and fly is to heal.

May this book inspire others to walk this journey, to heal and set themselves free, so that they too can enjoy the present, by releasing the wounds and stepping towards the light.

CHAPTER TWO

23/10/18 MY DREAM

In my dream I had horses appear. Horses are something that have had deep significance for me; they were an absolute love in my life for many, many years.

I have been drawn to Native American art, teachings, and their reverence for the animal kingdom in particular. Horses symbolise 'personal power' and they came into my life, for real, to support me in one of the toughest times in my life. For man and male has been a heavily loaded influence in my life and every single relationship I have had to date has been heartbreaking and horrific.

I write this chapter with my son, yes my son, sitting beside me on the sofa that is my place of choice to write. He is playing a Wii game and he is sitting crossed legged, his knee is touching my thigh, as we are sitting close. He is jabbering away about the game and involves me in every section of his adventuring. I can look to my left and see his gentle eyes, I can see his soft young cheek that readily changes shape when he smiles. He does not know how to savage somebody with brutal words, he knows not how to control someone and take away any shred of hope or self-worth. He has kindness coming out of every single sound. He looks at me with love, he readily tells me he loves me. He gives to me, with no shred of the intent and intentions of others. He is kind, he is male.

Horses to me were just the same. At the age of sixteen I developed ME and, at the mid-point in my healing of this illness, I finally got my wish to have a horse. It was a poorly one from a rescue centre that needed lots of TLC and I was ready to give it. For as long as I can remember, I have been drawn to horses; the financial situation at home meant I couldn't but with my gradual improvement of health I started to do small hours at a local factory and hence the horse appeared in my life. His name was Penri (he was the poorly one mentioned above). Eventually he was homed elsewhere as when he became fit, he became too much for a novice rider like myself.

So, I loaned horses and rehabilitated more for the centre, and eventually I came to the place of owning a lovely cob called Joe, who developed arthritis in the knee and was unrideable. What he taught me in this journey with him was total strength of character and willpower for he defeated the odds regarding his medical condition and oozed this energy of sheer 'presence in the now'.

He commanded respect and was the boss of every horse I ever had with him, even with the arthritis and discomfort, respect was his. Yet because I couldn't ride him, I began the search for a horse to do this with.

I came upon, or life delivered me, a permanent loan of a horse called Harry. Even writing his name here I have tears in my eyes; he was something else. I have always bonded with animals but with him it was on another level. I could let him free graze anywhere on the farm, and all I would need to do was call his name and he would whinny to me; I would then know where he was.

I knew he would not stray. He would look at me with such love, and when I rode him I had peace but also this stream of love coming from him to me. He touched my heart and kept it pumping when I had such pain in my life. My father and men, man, were ripping me to shreds.

How does an animal come to mean so much? He was sent by that which guides us all, that which gives us enough light to keep our heads and hearts up. I am hugely thankful for this being in my life. He taught me the strength in being gentle; he was a big horse, yet he was so soft. His muzzle was like velvet, his eyes the softest brown and his hair was like silk.

I started doing my shamanic retreats when I had him and every single time I went away he went downhill. Something would happen, he would become miserable and end up lame or injured. He would be waiting for me to come home.

Then, on his passing, during the weeks before he left this earth, animal communication came through thick and fast. He would stream this other world to me, the one that is around us and yes within us. How do I know this? Because it felt like home.

Why was he sent? Because I needed him. My father developed an inoperable heart condition and, very soon on the wake of this illness, he had a nervous breakdown. He was a man that worked his farm, that was it, and when he couldn't do that, he broke.

What happened was a dip into silence but a silence that was so heavy it suffocated you. He tried to hang himself on numerous occasions. He was admitted into a mental health hospital and was medicated.

I visited him soon after his admission and, as we

sat, I noticed his shoes were soaking wet. I looked at this quiet man, this man who didn't look in your eyes, this man that looked lost. I went to sort out his shoes, find dry slippers and socks, and I mentioned to the staff about his wet shoes. What came to light was that he had tried to drown himself in the hospital, fully clothed. They found the rest of his things dripping wet.

He came home, silent, completely and utterly. Like a cloak that covered the whole house, you could feel it when you entered. He lay on the sofa, then went to bed; that was it. We had a pet budgie and we had to rehome him as he got depressed too, being in the same space as my father.

The silence stayed.

CHAPTER THREE

MY FATHER

My father's physical health was poor also. The heart condition left him with a weak body, his back began to bend from lack of muscle use, plus arthritis was setting in. He walked on two sticks.

I was washing my car one day and, as I was doing so, my father slowly walked past; this bent over, quiet man, crossed the yard of the farm, opened the door to the barn and walked in.

I continued washing my car, but as I was washing the outside mirror, a little spider was on it. I looked at this small spider, and he told me. He told me to go to my father.

As I walked into the barn, what I saw was my bent over, weak father had managed to pull a small straw bale under a low beam in the barn roof.

He had a length of bale twine in his hands and

had managed to get an end of it over the beam. He saw me, he said nothing, I saw him and said nothing.

He dropped the string and slowly walked past me, he went back into the house and we called the mental health hospital and he was re-admitted.

This happened, this was a moment in my life, a moment where I listened to a tiny spider, a moment when Spirit worked through this being and delivered a message to me. For without it my father would have left this world with baler twine around his neck and the last thing he would have seen was an empty barn.

For years after, I questioned this moment. Should I have stopped him, as my father suffered with his mind for so many years after? It was later that it came to light that his will was not sufficient and, if he had left this earth then, my mother would have lost the farm. The farm she had worked like a dog on too, the thing she had fought to keep and which she needed as her health was fading as well.

So many times in life I have not known the reason why, but when a clear and guided message is given, I know I have to trust. For the voice of the spider did not scream, it was quiet, it was calm, it was clear. It saved my father, it saved the farm, it saved our memories of the farm itself. It saved my mother from poverty later in life and it meant that when my father did eventually lose his life, he did it with us, not on his own, hidden away. He went surrounded by our love and we felt his.

Trusting a message, trusting a sign, trusting in something more than myself and my current situation. Trust. Who is it that truly we lose trust in? I believe it is ourselves. We forget and disconnect from that deep inner knowing and inner voice that is connected to everything and everyone.

When we disconnect from this inner truth, we then stop trusting ourselves. We are more easily swayed by the opinions of others and so feel less trustworthy.

The spider who showed me the way at such a critical time had the good of all at its core; all. So too do we, when we regain that path of trust; the realisation that at our core WE KNOW we are connected. The spider connected as deeply with me as any human being.

28/10/18

As I walk this path with writing this book, I have absolutely no idea where it is going, what I will say, how big it will be and even its title. All I know is this: it feels like home when I am here doing it, and when

THE MASK

I step away and resist it feels like a pressure building up inside of me that cannot be released any other way. This is what I am meant to be doing RIGHT NOW, it is as simple as that.

CHAPTER FOUR

WHO AM I?

My son has recently opened up to the world of films and we are loving the journey of *Kung Fu Panda*. It has everything for us both. I love the wisdom that is entwined in the story, my son loves the hero and the 'good against evil' in it.

I am walking the path of self-discovery, which started a long time ago, whilst my son is learning about the duality of life. Wrapped up in a story that is written by another, there are always threads of learning for all.

There are times when my story feels more like me than the actual truth of who I am. Even now writing this I feel tension, I feel this unease as I sit and write, where are my words going to take me? What memories are going to jump out and get me? What bogey monster is going to rise up and hijack this whole book and the meaning of it? What?

For, as with all things, it is fear that hold us back, our yesterdays and our tomorrows, the fear of what was and what will be. Fears. All my mind is saying, whispering and screaming is "control". Do something or make something happen to control this moment. Do something that I have power to control, so that it will take my mind off stepping outside of my comfort zone and truly connecting with the process as this book unfolds.

It came up for me today as I got up, after a peaceful sleep. I have my period right now and it takes me every time to the fire place of release, the place that is set aside for wonderful things to happen. "Release that which holds you back" she whispers, this amazingly powerful cycle of womanhood, that comes to my body, and gives me exactly what I need every single month.

For, if I have pushed myself too much, she will whisper "rest", if I have not been honest with my emotions throughout the month, she will say "cry" or "allow anger"; she knows and it is at these times I am most receptive to the 'inner voice'.

So today as I woke and I bled she offered up 'control'. Releasing the need for it and the automatic response of the mind which does its best to control absolutely everything in and around myself.

However, the control comes with a history; it has the voice of all my pain and wounds. My past is hidden in the word 'control', it's woven into every letter. 'Limit the damage to myself', the voice of the mind says, but actually what it's doing is keeping me in a box.

Am I truly this? A woman in a box? Confined by the mind voice, the one that seeks to keep me safe? Perhaps. But what rules are governing this voice? Ones from the past. There is no softness or allowing to this voice, there is only rigidity and obedience. No kindness or humour, only self-preservation and inner imprisonment.

For my mind has done its very best to control things around me, and in turn drawn those who would control me walking through the door. My mind's idea of controlling things to keep me safe only ended up bringing exactly the experiences and people who were anything but safe. What is put out comes back. The idea of keeping safe comes from the fear-based platform, it was not built on love, but was laid brick by brick with fear. So, the fear only attracted that which it was trying to avoid.

An unsafe world, with unsafe people, who would do me harm, who would use and abuse me. Welcome one and all! Is that who I am? NO. There comes a time when, after removing people from your life, situations, hell even social media is taken off your phone, when everything is removed, at the final realisation when there is nothing more to remove, the 'inner voice' says "look inside".

My head is not who I am, my mind carries records and keeps account of all my wrong doings, my head then creates a set of rules to live by, a set of rules that are implanted in my life, based on every single past hurt. It is then laid in front of my eyes and the mind says "this is the truth, this is who other people are, this is who you are, live from the framework of the past, walk its well-trodden path, stay safe, let no one truly in". This is not who I am.

Who am I? I am the one in that quiet space inside, I am the one who hears voices from spiders, I am the one who jumps for joy inside at the autumn leaves, I am the one who marvels at the sight of white feathers on my path as I take a walk.

I am the one who fills with absolute awe at the sight of my son, the miracle that came out of my body, that grew in my womb and inspires me. I am the one who when I look into the mirror and really look into my eyes, I see this stillness, this peace, this knowing. This is who I am. This connection with all things, wonder at all things.

I am not my past, *there is no one to blame.*

What keeps the past alive and controlling me?

What keeps the mind voice so strong? Blame.
So much is written and spoken about forgiveness, the importance of it, to truly be free. Yet until I come to the place of releasing blame, I am locked, locked in the world of counting the wrongdoings and by whom. The book of wrongdoings to self. It is a weighty book that smells fusty, like the old mouldy books that have been in the cellar for so many years that they have taken on the aroma of that which was around them. It is like the proverbial witch's book of spells, containing the power to hold the owner of it in lock down. Held, by shackles that are unbreakable, to the past.

I had one of those letters come in the post, 'Have you ever been mis-sold PPI? If so, we can search for free and claim it back for you'. I sent it off and forgot about it. Yesterday the letter came back saying I hadn't put enough information in the letter to allow them to contact any relevant companies. I gave thanks and put the letter in the bin, for 'there is no one to blame'. For whilst I am searching for someone or something to lay the blame on, I am trapped in the witch's spell book of the past, shackled to the web of pain, keeping count, and staying completely stuck to the past.

There is a time to totally and utterly fume at what has happened. There is a time to release every single emotion attached to a situation or person. There is a time to be completely and utterly floored by the injustice of a trauma. There is a time for that and if you cannot have the time to do so when the pain occurs then YOU MUST do it later on. Whether that is days, weeks, months or years afterwards, YOU MUST.

When you have felt, when you have allowed yourself to be completely overwhelmed and taken over by the releasing, then and only then do you step into the open door of 'there is no blame'.

Why? For peace. There is a Native American saying that for every finger you point at someone two comes back. My feeling and interpretation of this is that the finger we point at another eats away at us; for how long do we hold the finger up at someone? How much energy does it take to do so? And we lose the use of a hand with the pointing, we lose part of us, and cannot function wholly until we bring the hand down to our side again and release the finger that is pointing. Only then can we be free of what was.

The weight of the 'witch's spell book' of keeping records of the blame is so off the scale. It is not the Filofax of notes, neatly written in as few words as possible. It is the biggest, heaviest book you can possibly imagine, and it weighs us down until we open it and, one by one, read through the list of names and events. No amount of running, of hiding, of business, of control, of causes to fight for, of others people's lives we get involved in instead of our own, there is *no distraction that can keep us from this book.*

It is here waiting for you, the person reading these words. It is waiting. Read it.

CHAPTER FIVE

RUNNING

Oh, how I have run. I would love to say it has been some useful running that had a purpose, like those athletes who run marathons. No, I have not run a single one, but inside I have been running for most of my life.

Deep inside there is this pit of fear, driven, fed and kept alive by my mind, the mind that has held all the records of my life history. For my mind has been like the well-known elephant that never forgets. I have run with this fear inside of me, I have been the ultimate employee, ploughing into a task, completing it and pushing myself to the limit to get a job done. I can multitask to the max. I can bolt down my food without barely tasting it and boy oh boy can I get involved in other people's lives.

Sound like anyone you know? Sound like you?

Causes, there are so many and they all have so much good they are doing. They are also a great vehicle to hitch a ride on when you are running, for no one will even know and you can even kid yourself. The cause then becomes a vehicle to pour all those anxious feelings that are surfacing, the ones telling you to stop, but you can't as there is this great cause that needs you.

I could start a massive project, just as those feelings surface and say "it's time to stop the running and face the witch's spell book"; the call will keep coming, so I can release, be free of the spell book, and guess what? Start a brand new book, one where the pages are blank, they are infused with love, they have flower essences seeping from each page, morning dew is on every corner, so we have the moisture to turn each page and peace is written in invisible handwriting so there is plenty of room for your own words. It is waiting.

Me? What has stopped me? Right now? Today? Money and, more to the point, lack of it. The world of juggling funds, of not being able to do and go places. Another form of stopping the running, for I cannot pay to go, to do, to move.

My current situation financially, which has to be opened and acknowledged, is of being in debt. The joy of modern money moving has meant I have an overdraft with my bank AND a credit card transfer; the modern magic of hiding the truth, until it can no longer be hidden, until it has an impact on life and family. Yet this too is part of the process.

There have been so many times Spirit has called and I have yes let something come to light, a part of my history would suddenly pop right in front of my face; I would stop and look, do the work, but I have still run on. I have remembered, healed, released, stepped forward and run like hell again.

My process has been the one of peeling the layers of an onion; this experience came up, I felt, I faced, I released, I healed. The time of peace, joy and then another layer, same process, different past experience. Many years and many lessons, tools, tears and gifts.

The path of awareness. Of open eyes and continuing to keep them open, means feeling, really feeling.

Every time I released, a deeper layer came forward.

Today I sit with my laptop, I have been stopped from running, I can't with no money. I have had my times of physical illness, for that is another one of the ways to stop us running. When our physical body stops us, it's a big call to listen to what's inside. It is in seeing beyond the diagnosis, the illness, the medication that there is, then the opportunity to step inside and let your spell book go.

I have also had my time of caring for others, for again this one can be maxed out on the path of running; by absolutely putting everything into someone else, you have well and truly run, and hidden in them, where the self-sacrifice can be hidden in the realms and respectability of being a 'carer'. It goes unnoticed that you aren't actually caring for yourself whilst doing it, yet it is the tell-tale sign of the running path. For there are a million and one ways of running without actually moving an inch, let alone a mile.

I have employed and deployed just about every way of running the path. I have worked on myself but then run again. From jobs, relationships, illness, caring for others, and now I visit another path, debt. For one thing, I have learnt that it can be an amazing vehicle to pour all my anxiety into. It also has the ability to stop me going out, treating myself, buying clothes, food, living. It has stopped me in my tracks, why? Because it was the one thing that would, for also part of my running path means I am a fighter.

If life gets tough, I stand up and fight. If things are difficult, I go headlong at it. I have a brain that can plan, organise, sort, get things done. I have been known for so long as the one people turn to as I know what to do and how to do it. I can handle things. I can see how to overcome something.

So, Spirit has given me something that cannot be overcome by anything I have in my toolkit to date, and for all this time I have been trying to find ways to get out and it has only got deeper. My hole is so deep that now I can no longer prise myself out with any kind of physical strength at all. I had four days last month where I went over my overdraft limit and I had absolutely no money to get from anywhere to change it, so every day I had a text message alert that I would get a fee for every single day, a standard fee. I sat at home, saw the texts and STOPPED. I had nowhere to go.

I have worked, oh I have worked, I have prayed, I have thought outside the box, I have read, I have talked to people. Worked on my unhealthy beliefs about money, listened to positive meditations on abundance, said the affirmations to then be in exactly the same situation, with funds lacking and the feeling of dread inside at each bill to pay.

I finally did a spiritual surrender, I finally admitted "I don't know", I don't know what to do, where to go, what I am meant to be doing and with whom. I don't know, and in those words something clicked. The control mind had no purchase in this domain, combined with the inability to do, by my finances, it has led me to this place and space.

"I don't know" Is one of the greatest tools to be used on the mind who is desperate for control. It takes it into a realm it has no data on and in that realm the inner wisdom can come forward and guide us to the lessons to release in our old spell book, crammed with the past.

The two lessons thus far have been the understanding and liberation of 'there is no one to blame' and the antidote to the controlling mind of 'I don't know'. For all the beautiful music and wise words that can be found on the internet, and in books, it is only by our stopping that we can hear *our own words.*

We all need to understand that, for every crisis, for every trauma, for every single thing that is happening to us right now, somewhere there is an inner you that is calling, that is supporting and encouraging us to stop, to listen, to be guided and to *remember* who we truly are. For we are not what has happened or is happening to us, we are so much more. We are the magic that we see in a rainbow, the beauty in our children's smiles, the joy in a dew drop, the majesty of the highest mountain and the serenity of the morning sun that is so gentle, so full of hope and that lights our lives. We are all of that which we love, for when our eyes marvel at something on this earth, it is showing us *ourselves*. For we are all things, we are connected to everything, everything.

Our current situation is here to help us, however horrendous it may seem; it is here to stop us, to heal us, to release us from our past.

CHAPTER SIX

HEALING

There is that age old quote that gets bandied around: "everything happens for a reason". It has stood the test of time because it is the way forward and a truly valuable tool on the self-healing path.

When we are in the midst of a crisis, when the world seems to crash around your ears, it is the last thing you will think of and neither should you, for you are in the moment with whatever is going on around you. But afterwards, when the crisis is over, when red alert has passed, then the words can support you on the path of release and healing.

Recently, when my son was getting our family dog back in from the garden he shut his thumb in the door. He held his thumb and he cried, for he felt it, no holding back, no holding in, it hurt! I did not suppress his cries, for they are that which is a pure and true release, of being in the moment. That hurt, he felt it, he expressed it, it's now over. He may have a mark on his thumb and require a plaster, but it's done, it leaves no effect or build up inside of him.

That is a simple example, it is the "don't cries" that are said around us, not for the welfare of the person upset but because our crying is upsetting the other person, their need to fix the pain. Why are we all so afraid of expressing pain, even when it really hurts?

Children are surrounded by these comments, they are accused of acting up, boys are encouraged to be strong and don't cry, or told by an adult "that's enough", when it so clearly isn't.

It may be enough for the adult hearing it, as they are being limited by their own lack of expression, so expect the child to conform and conform they will. When they are told something enough times, they start to believe it. Here starts the pressure cooker of unexpressed emotions, and from here on in they build the unfelt and unexpressed deep inside.

How do I know? Because I have and continue to work with every voice, opinion and constraint that was around me when I was growing up, because I have learnt and am continuing to learn what is real and what is someone else's programme planted in my mind.

5/11/18

My son went back to school today, after two weeks on holiday. For me it was two weeks with a little lad that demonstrated yet again how much he has grown, how much he has grown out of.

We did the sorting of toys and clothes, and saw all the things that he wasn't playing with anymore, the things he had loved for so long, relegated to a box hidden away, or in a heap. With my assistance, he looked at things and decided what he wanted to keep and what he wanted to let go of. With complete clarity and certainty, he let go of so many things; I admire the non-attachment. That which was once loved has served its purpose and he lets go. I wish to harness more of that energy myself.

As I walk my path, I too have grown, and with that growth comes change. Yet I hold on, afraid to let go. As an adult, the very thought of letting go brings a range of emotions from mild anxiety to terror.

I have learnt how to work hard, how to fight, how to struggle, how to keep going when my back's against the wall. To rise to every challenge and beat it, to be strong, to be planning the next stage. In there is absolutely nothing about letting go, and yet in order to make space for the new it's so important.

To allow softness instead of the harder energy

of my 'pushing through obstacles', to allow flow instead of control and to allow trust instead of absolute mistrust. I have quite honestly felt completely overwhelmed, as letting go has felt like an area I know absolutely nothing about. Welcome to the world of "I don't know".

In many ways, those three words have become a healing balm for me recently, when my head does its chatter, when someone asks me a question about my work, my life, but mostly when my mind does its talk. I answer with "I don't know", and then the peace washes over me.

This weekend I took my son to a birthday party. There were climbing walls, and after the children had had their turn the adults were allowed to have a go. There were different types of walls to climb and a harness around each person with a rope that you were attached to. I found it easy to climb but it was the sitting back and trusting in the harness that I couldn't get my head around, trusting that this harness was there for me, that this rope would hold and that I wouldn't come crashing to the floor when I let go.

This is somewhere where we all come to rest at some stage in our lives, when a trauma, an illness, a life change comes to our door, when the dust settles on our way of being and doing. We climb, we work, we strive and then suddenly it's the time to 'allow'; we sit back and trust in the presence of something in our lives. A force, a being, a faith, an energy, something more than us, but also part of us, something so immense it is everywhere, yet has the intelligence to ask with gentility to be part of our lives. No force, no screaming at us to listen, it is here waiting.

The second part of the birthday party, after the climbing walls, was a trampoline park and I threw myself into the whole experience, I became alive, alive with joy and that present moment feeling. An energy that felt boundless and limitless was within and around me, this joy for life, for living.

As we all contemplate our lives, our life mission, our point for being on this earth, wouldn't it be wonderful if we came from this place PERMANENTLY. The big questions of what we are meant to be doing, where we are meant to be going, would fall on the fertile ground of deep joy.

It was such a tonic for me, to feel this level of aliveness, and it gave me the total certainty that I want to live, to experience and to connect with myself and others on this level.

I have read how we have become a goal-driven society, so much so that we are never truly living in the present, and are always looking to the future.

What is happening right now for you? As you are reading these words?

For myself, I am sitting at the kitchen table, meditation music playing. The house feels empty after two weeks of my son's presence; I miss him. As I acknowledge this moment right now, the house quiet of his chatter, his energy and my role as mum has slipped away until 3.30pm when I pick him up. It is here I sit, in the energy of just me. Who am I?

CHAPTER SEVEN

WHO AM I NOW?

With tears in my eyes, I am feeling the reality of this moment, this non-mother mode, this mode and role I love so very much. Thanks to this tiny bundle of joy who came into my world in 2010, my heart burst with love and I became that which I have always dreamed of, a mum.

As a child I remember putting my pet cat to my nipple; in the pretend world of a young child, I was breastfeeding, my ginger and white cat Trixie being the substitute baby. If anyone asked me what my dream was, it was to be a mum. I remember as I got older and became a woman, I would look at my stomach and imagine what it would be like to have the baby bump. It finally became my reality when I was thirty-eight.

This child gave me the courage to really look at

my life and what was going on in it. For I knew that what I did not face, he would have to and I would be watching my son fighting battles I could have stopped. So, for the love of him, I faced so many painful truths, stood up to people, stepped away from situations and would not stay quiet. For history repeats itself and there is nothing like family history.

So, I stood, like I did on the weekend with the wall in front of me, and I found the footholds to climb each and every one. I would look at the challenge and whatever was the framework in front of me, whatever the task that had to be completed, and I did it.

I did it for the little eyes that followed my every move, the little heart that beat inside of me and then came from my body, the little arms that reached up to me and needed me; he needed me, he loved me. So, for him I scaled the walls, I scaled them all.

Now, right now, the walls are done, every single one, and I am here at the top of every single quest, every single challenge, and I am expected to what?

I don't know who I am. The strongest I have ever been is for that boy, for my son. Now all the monsters are laid to rest and the demons are destroyed, my son's path is clear and he walks forward into this world. Now I ask, who am I?

The mother role is allowing space now. It is

stepping aside for the woman to step forward. I know I must accept, trust and allow the nothingness, the "I don't know", to settle.

My mind has been working overtime recently. I understand now it's been looking for the next battle, the next demon to slay, the challenge, and it hasn't found any. It has tried to fool me so many times, it has tried to lay traps for me, by laying a plan down in front of my eyes, a trap, conning me into believing that holy hell was on its way again. Truth is, I know it's not, I can feel it's done. Oh, I know I am human and will be continuing to work on myself for the rest of my life, but I know the path clearing is done.

I feel this truth about these words and, in a way, it scares the pants off me. Eight years of intense clearing, removing people, situations, places, and most of all healing of myself, so I did not pass on history to my son. Now it is done. Now I know I can breathe and I can allow myself to expand again and follow my heart. For my heart tells me to step into the world, to expand, to become part of it again.

So, I sit in this empty house, listen to my meditation music, write these words and weep, for I know it's time to face the void. The battles are over, my child is growing, he is spreading his wings, and all the space he filled inside of me, as I lived the mother role to the max, it's past. Oh, I know it starts again when I pick him up, it's just different now, the intensity of the younger years is over. It's done.

The time when it is you and only you they need, the time when they could be picked up and cuddled, completely cuddled, for they are these bundles of pure love, that look to you for everything and want for nothing. Their needs are met by you, they are surrounded by love and their world is YOU.

I have so loved this world, after a lifetime of wanting to be a mother, a miscarriage years ago, and finally having this little lad enter my life and my heart. I now have to find the light within, to find the love within, so I can follow my own joy, live my own life and beam my own light. He has given me so much, he made me question my life and everyone in it, he gave me courage and now I must find my own path again.

After all the hard work, who am I? Nothing makes sense. I look at all I have done and it feels and is the past; my art work, my healing work, this nothingness. This is where I need to be and right now accept, don't fight it, or seek for it to be anything else. I have read there is a time for everything, a time to be happy, a time to be sad, a time to be tired, etc. This is my time for nothingness, I do not have the heart or the energy to climb walls, which is why I know the challenges are behind me. I have nothing left.

6/11/18

Everywhere is perfect, the perfect life on Facebook, magazines, all is perfect. Where is the real? I am hurting, yet where are the people expressing their hurt? Are they all too afraid to share their hurt because of the wave of perfect that is sweeping over our society? Where are the grieving mothers, who honour and respect this rite of passage? From the deep parenting role to the emerging woman phase.

My concern for us all is that, in a time when we can actually share our truths without a system clamping down on us, we have actually created a clamp ourselves with the over positive. Has this not become another silencer? For it only leaves room for one single thing, for one vehicle and avenue of expression – that which is most pleasing to all and that which can be the ultimate tombstone to the soul.

To live in only one aspect of self, when we have a huge range of emotions, which are neither right or wrong and should not be labelled as such, they just are. The reason we have so many of them is simple: we are meant to!

My child has taught me that, for he has expressed whatever the emotion is at the time he was feeling it. It is us adults who become disconnected from our true emotions, by suppressing and resisting our true feelings/emotions. Why do we resist now? For all that we have learnt and had thrust upon us as children actually has no hold over us now as adults, we have the right to choose. We can choose.

I can choose to be authentic; we can choose to be real, we can choose to express things at the time, and if we feel unable to express at the time, at least acknowledge to ourselves how we are actually feeling and not judge it.

SILENCE

The ultimate killer of our bodies, our minds and our hearts is silence. It is also the ultimate weapon, which keeps us locked to an old experience or person, in another world and held ransom to our pasts. Silence.

What have you been silent about dear reader? And why? Were you afraid of what others would say or do to you? It is the very weapon that abusers, bullies and users depend on to keep us under control; silence.

Then those who have been abused carry the

words "don't say anything" in their minds and it stays with them and haunts them for the rest of their lives, until they confront their pasts and those who planted the silence inside of them.

Are you one of those people, dear reader? Are you one of those pretending that everything is fine? Showing the world and yourself that all is 'perfect'? I know, as I have been that person most of my life, I know the silence. I know the feeling of living in a flat world, where only limited emotions are accepted and acceptable, I know the restrictions and the emptiness that eats away at you. I also know the web of lies this world is built upon.

I have had all the labels: abused, assaulted, bullied, used and controlled. It was a massive part of my life. Living under restrictions and then finally starting the process of stepping out of those roles, healing and loving myself enough to never visit those places again, to never allow those energies and people into my mind and my life.

Blame was my greatest silencer. It is a clever trick to have been encouraged to use on myself by others, but ultimately, I took the mantle on myself and it was that feeling that kept me locked in my own silence. It is the greatest tragedy, that whatever is done to us, if it really hurts us, it gets deep inside us and worms its way into our very fabric of being.

I took on the role of blame, and blamed myself for everything that happened and, in doing so, it was so easy for others to hook into this mindset. I made it so easy for them all, my default button would go to "it's my fault". Job done.

However, a web that is created by others to silence us, to keep us in our place and to keep us controlled, can be woven a new way. How? By seeing the beauty of this image, that we can create our very own web, free from those who did us harm. How to do this? Feel.

CHAPTER EIGHT

WHERE TO BEGIN

You begin right now, in acknowledging how you are feeling in this moment, and the next, and the next. Just admit to yourself how you feel; this is the start of becoming aware, allowing yourself full expression and allowing all the parts of you that have been suppressed to have a voice. Memory Lane, for you, will follow and allow it to happen. Allow yourself to 'go within', this is your journey to reclaim your now and heal the past.

No one has the right to silence you, no one, and no one can open up the lines to inner communication again except you. No one can make it real for you, no one can thaw the numbness inside, except you. This is your ultimate gift to self.

Right now, for me, everything feels empty; my house, my heart. I look around at my kitchen, my son's paintings are on every door, every surface of the cupboards and fridge. His photos are looking at me, hanging from a plastic wall hanger; him in the snow, him with his dog, us two together; and how I feel when I look at those photos is relief. He hasn't had my childhood, he smiles in every single photo, he smiles. I feel proud and relieved to have got to this place, but also tired.

Looking at the photos I remember so very much, looking into his eyes I see light and happiness, oh he will have his own personal journey in life, but he will not have mine and my family's. I also know without a shadow of a doubt, that my life would have carried on the same path if I had not had my son. It was him that gave me the strength to go within, it was him who made me see the truth and do something about it. How can things not change when your life is touched by unconditional love?

I do not know where to start and what to say about my past; there has been so much that has happened, so much to heal, so much to let go of and so much fear to face. I am asking myself right now, what actually needs to be said and what do others need to read, as my words can be a road map for others to follow, to give encouragement and courage to those willing to heal the past.

So, I allow the words to flow onto this page, and

I share what I am meant to. It hurts in the writing, for I make things real. I remember and honour where I have been and how much I have been through.

Everything I write are the experiences wrapped up in silence, the "don't say anythings", and it's hard, sitting here on my fence, having been there, done it and got the tee shirt. Now here on the cusp of sharing to support others, I could so easily stay on the fence. Who wants to hear this and, most importantly of all, who will get hurt by my sharing? But those who will feel this are already eaten away by a pain so deep that it affects every aspect of their lives and they are totally ruled by their past and their pain. So, I step up, for every brave being who wishes to heal.

I have taken my dog for a walk before I continued with writing this. There is a resistance to taking this step. I take a walk around the estate where I live. It's quiet today and I am thankful for this space and place for it supports me.

There are two paths to take, the path where I tell you exactly what happened, or the path where I lead you on the recovery route. I hereby choose recovery, for the details are my story and they are deep, but they are mine.

There has not been a time, that I can remember,

when I was not easy to control. It was so easy for the bullies to bully me, the controllers to control me and the manipulators to manipulate me. This was my path and I knew nothing different. Until a catastrophic incident that changed the course of my life.

9/11/18

I was assaulted by a family member and, because of this, it opened up a deep wound that needed to heal, for it wasn't just mine, it was a family line, a family history. So, for something that ripped me to pieces, I am truly thankful, because this violation made me question everything that I viewed as normal and it made me look at my past, where I came from, and it helped me uncover the truth.

Like all children, I accepted and absorbed everything that was around me, and as an adult it has had an impact on my life deeply, without questioning the source and course of my life. Now I question everything and so should we all. Question why you are afraid of something, why you react to certain things. What you believe and why. Is it your belief? Truly yours, is it really your own thoughts? Or are they learnt behaviours and, without realising it, we have morphed into parrots that just copy what has been said to us?

For each of us has to empty our minds of all learnt beliefs and refill our cups with self-love, wonder and hope for ourselves and this world. I have a child that is in this world and I wish to make my mark on this life so it improves for us all.

Abuse is fed and kept alive by silence, by fear of speaking and the grooming of our minds by the very families that have suffered the most and are so trying to protect us. But, when they have not healed themselves, they unwittingly pass on the mantle to future generations. For they carry the guilt and silence in their being, in their bones, in their cells, in their words and in their hearts.

They, with all the love and wish to protect, actually make us the easiest to be used and abused. Fear does not need words, it spreads like the plague, for no rats are required to pass it on, it has no limits. It is our hearts that have the only antidote: self-love. I ask and plead with you all, those who have been abused, look to your hearts and commit 100% to self-love. You have to, you deserve a better life and so do your children.

No one tells you the truth, no one holds the space better for you than YOU. No one tells you that you have the programme inside of you and, unless you heal, you pass on this faulty programme to your children.

Yes, you can prosecute those who hurt you, yes you can cut them from your life, yes you can try to bury the truth, pretend it never happened, deny all knowledge, blank them all from your life. But unless you heal, it is all there in your memory bank, stored under lock and key. But also it is where you come from with every word, every thought, for it is your base and it will affect every aspect of your life. It rots away at your trust, your energy, your view of life and love and it will be waiting for you, until you are ready to heal.

Feel, just allow feelings. As one example of acknowledging the past and its effect, I will share one simple memory and its effect on myself.

There has been for myself an attraction to men with alcohol on their breath. It is something that for years has baffled me completely, as it is not a natural instinct or response, yet for me it has become one. Why? From before I was born until I was nine or ten, there was a live-in farm worker at my home, and he was an alcoholic; what compounded it and made it normal for me was that I have so few memories of him. He controlled and bullied my mother, yet because my father worked on the family farm from dawn until dusk, this alcoholic man would have been the main male in the home.

There is a reason why I have blanked him out. It is only three years ago that I was told how long he had lived with us, and it was such a shock, as I only have a couple of memories of the role he has played in my life. This is what happens to children.

Wake up all of us, for it is not about filling our children's rooms with toys and jetting them off to fantastic places, it is about filling their lives with love and positive role models. If they do have to spend time around negative influences, then you make sure you carry the truth inside of you.

Do the homework, work on yourself, do not carry into the home every single person who has done you harm, for until you heal, they sit down at the table with you and your child. They are the ghosts of your past, that can speak through you when you get pushed, when you get upset and when you get scared.

You want to give your child a gift? Give them an authentic parent, give them the parent who is working on themselves and healing their pasts.

The best table in the world is the one where only you and your loved ones are present. Look around right now, look at your table, who is there? If you want to know if it's only you, then stop, grow silent and look inside. For if you feel uncomfortable in the silence of self, then there is something and someone knocking on your internal door. Invite them in, or they will continue to be the unwelcome guest at your dinner table. They will jump out of your mouth the next time your child pushes your buttons, and they will speak, not you, and the cycle will continue.

Having a child opens up the door to our own childhoods; now you know why part of you wants to run back to the life before you had them. They have been sent to you, and are asking you to heal your past.

How do you know someone or a situation has been healed? When you can forgive, with honesty and peace, forgive. Until then, those who aren't forgiven reside inside of you, the acts that they performed, the words they said and the wounds they inflicted will not heal.

However crazy busy you get, they will still be inside of you, however much food you eat, however much sex you have and with whom, they are still there. You will attract people like them, the negativity that is held will have a hold over you. You will expect less from life, accept the job you hate, put up with negative friends, unhappy situations and a low expectation of what life can offer.

Forgiving is for us, not for them, forgiving is so

we can be free; those who hurt were hurting, those who abused us were abused. They have their path but it does not have to be a path we share with them any longer. Separate your path from them, make it your own, learn where you have come from, so you can heal, then find out who you truly are. Be free.

There is so much I wish to say to you, to give you courage, hope and faith in yourself, just know this; you have to do this work to allow yourself the gift of a heart that pumps with love. A heart that has no restrictions and a heart that then passes on this gift to your children.

So much is said about the influences of the outside world on our children, and of course there are many, but the deepest impact on a child's life is who we have at our table. Who we invite in, the ones buried in our silence, the ones buried in our fears, the ones we have to forgive.

My parents loved me, of that I am 100% certain, my father in Spirit and my mother on this earth, they love me. They had both been hurt so very much that so many ghosts came to the family table, and there became too little room for the living. Fear was the constant and fear allowed people into the home that should never have passed over the threshold. For our ghosts normalise that which is not normal, and attracts those with a similar vibration.

THE MASK

There is a weeding out going on in my mind, for myself; normal and not have become mixed up.

I actually feel uncomfortable around genuine people, I mistrust them and go straight into the unhealthy. So, I am learning to be incredibly uncomfortable around decent people, resisting the urge to pull away from them, shut the door and pull the curtains shut. In doing so I have seen those it's important to weed out of my life, with the most shocking of behaviour, which I accepted as normal.

The reversal has interested me, and I invite you all to see what your mental pattern is, acknowledge it and face it. I do not blame others, for the toxic people I allowed into my life I let in.

My past may have made them seem familiar, but it was still me who opened the door to them and my life. They showed me who they were from the start; it was just so 'normal' for me that it felt like home. Because, for a big part of my life, it was. It was.

As I said, we now have the chance to weave our own web, to make it clear of our pasts and invite only love and loving people to our dinner table.

CHAPTER NINE

FEELINGS

The key to healing and releasing is *feeling*. Allowing yourself to feel, whatever it is, without labelling it as good or bad; for when we label it, we restrict it and hold on to it. We have all grown up with a set of beliefs about what is acceptable and what isn't, what is good and what is bad.

So what if the labels have been put on the wrong jars, so what if the strawberry jam got mixed up with the dog food? What if we have been told that the thing we should never touch, let alone eat, was just another flavour of jam? What if it was never dog food at all, it was just another jam, but the compounding of an idea by many affected your mind so you believe it to be true; so much so that you will never go to the jar, let alone admit it's in your cupboard.

3/12/18

Yesterday I put up the Christmas tree with my son. We went and bought a real one, got the decorations down from the attic and set the tone for the day. My son stood on a chair so he could place all the pieces on the tree, and the memory lane walk unfolds.

Some of the decorations, from years gone by, he has painted, cut, glittered and glued; the most unique exquisite creations. I remember each one and treasure the memory as he slips them on the branches of the tree. There are pieces I have bought, but mostly there are baubles and the like from my childhood, from my childhood home. I share the history with my son. As he places each piece, he says how beautiful they are, and they truly are. Parts of my life came alive as we co-created our Christmas tree.

It was a truly cheery day, we put on Christmas Carols, we met my mother and brother for lunch and the day ended with us brushing and hoovering all the pine needles up, happy with our home filled with festive cheer.

Today I feel this emptiness and a chasm opens up. I felt this pull to not send my son to school, to have his cheery energy around filling the house, but I let him go. I let him go.

So much has happened since I last put words on this page. My mother had the news her cancer had returned and for me it opened up a floodgate of emotions, and that has been my journey these past few weeks.

Actually allowing emotions, no matter what they are, without naming or shaming myself, just feeling. Being honest with people. For if they asked how I was feeling I would speak the truth.
What a healing that has been, to allow myself to be vulnerable with others; for in my past vulnerability was seen as a weakness and used by others.

A total and utter healing to just be, and in that being and allowing, I have found this peace, this quietness. I actually sat on the sofa, saw all the jobs there was to do and I stopped, I just sat and WAS. A stillness of body and mind, something I cannot remember experiencing.

There have been days I have been so angry, so angry that I chopped a chair up and burnt it, I needed to do something with this intense rage. Then so hurt that my heart felt it was ripping to pieces, tears flowed, but it was the heart, oh how it hurt and I let it. And days when I have felt so exhausted it was as much as I could do to get my son to school. These are the days that I share, the very real days, where emotions are allowed and respected, where there is nothing to stop them, for they are meant to come.

The gift of allowing the ripping apart, for wrapped up in my current life situation, which there is absolutely nothing I can do to make it better, I have dropped my mask.

As each piece of my unique mask showed itself to me and I was able to see it clearly for what it was, I could then lay down that piece and look at the next. The process is what I am sharing with you in this book, look at each past experience and let the hiding end.

For I had lived the life of the mask, the mask that shows others that everything is fine when it was the total opposite, and the worse it was the harder my mask was glued on. What a life not lived, no one truly knowing who I was, no one able to get in, and those I allowed in my life turned my emotions against me, so I pulled my mask on even harder.

My mother, the lady who gave birth to me, is being eaten alive, and I weep. Today I weep as I write because it is exactly what I need to give myself right now; tears. I do not question, I do not stifle them, I allow them. For I have fought too hard to squash my emotions and live in the narrow path of only allowing the 'nice' emotions to be expressed.

What an absolute prison and I, for one, will

never be silent again, will never hide my feelings for fear of others' disapproval. I am real and I am truly thankful that I am. I feel, at long last I truly connect with my feelings and allow them, at long last I am free.

I share this with you, as sometimes it takes the very worst thing to happen in your life for you to do the same. Something that for all the plans and control you implement in your daily life, you cannot stop; and when that comes, you open. Like my mother's illness, my father's passing or my assault by a family member.

Each experience jolted me out of my slumber, where I had become asleep to true aspects of myself. Suddenly I was brought something in my life that could not be ignored, I had to admit a truth, this really happened. Then healing steps in and I was shown what needed to be let go, dropping a piece of my mask.

I have had a number of profound experiences but they were needed as 'My Mask' was superglued on.

Open to the rawness, see it as a friend. The newness of real, real feelings, real expressing and real sharing with others are your path from here on in.

The conversations I have had with friends is only

deepening as I share, and show I am completely real and I feel. In amongst the days of tears and anger, I have days, hours or minutes of complete peace, for at last the reservoir of built-up emotions is set free.

I do not plan or think about what will happen, the journey that is ahead, for that unfolds a day at a time. I live, I love and I feel, that is my daily diet and the rest is in the hands of a greater power/force than mine.

It has taken my life being shot apart for the truth to be revealed. When I started this book, I was full of self-doubt about the process. How would I do it? What would I say? Would anyone buy it?

Now I see the greatest gift I can give myself and you who is reading this book, is the understanding that the truth and happiness that is our birth right is wrapped in each and every one of us removing our masks.

Whatever you fight for, whatever cause you are drawn to, whatever is happening in your life, look in the mirror and lay down your mask, see who you truly are and allow others the gift of seeing your truth.

The only way to light up this world is by seeing our own light. To do that, you have to lay to rest your mask.

AFTER

I share this journey so you all have the understanding of the process of regaining your truths. I share honestly so you all have the opportunity to acknowledge the wholeness of your life and its experiences.

It is in being honest and open I give you all the key to doing the same in your life, for there is no picture-perfect life. Those are just images, the truth lies in the whole of your life story, of which only you know it all and only you can heal.

Read these words and let your own mask slip away.

Many, many blessings.